...from the CoolREADS series...

A Handbook on How to Use Your Financial Statements to Manage Your Business

Understanding Your Financials: The Number One Determinant of Small Business Success

D1615758

By Jim Schell

Co-author of Small Business for Dummies

Copyright © 2017, Lights On Publishing. All rights reserved. No part of this book, including interior design and cover, may be reproduced or transmitted in any form, by any means, without the prior written permission of the author

For distribution information please call

Lights On Publishing
541-788-7137
Bend, Oregon

Printed in the United States of America

Contents

About the Author

Jim Schell writes about what he has lived. A graduate of the University of Colorado, Jim has been doing his small-business thing for 50 years. Over a 25-year Minneapolis career, Jim bootstrapped four businesses, one of which grew to 200 employees. After relocating to Central Oregon, he founded Opportunity Knocks, a peer-mentoring organization for teams of small business owners. Jim has written six books on small business including co-authoring *Small Business for Dummies.* He currently is down to owning one business, but is always on the prowl.

Jim's wife, Mary, is also the owner of a small business, a distribution company. Jim has three sons spread strategically across the U.S., so that wherever he goes, a grandchild cannot be far away. He and Mary reside in the hold-on-to-your-hat community of Bend, an outdoor playground disguised as a small town nestled in the high desert just east of the Cascade Mountain range. Two dozen golf courses lurk invitingly nearby.

Dedicated to the small business owner, our nation's #1 innovator and employer. May you enjoy success beyond your wildest dreams.

Introduction

It was a gray November morning when I received the phone call. "Jim," the female voice said softly. "I'm a small business owner and my business is having financial problems. Would you be willing to stop by my store and help me decide what to do next?"

It turns out I knew her retail business; I had shopped there. "Of course," I replied. "But I'll need to see your financial statements if I'm going to be able to help."

Later that afternoon I sat in her office, financial statements in hand. It took somewhere short of five minutes to check out her anemic balance sheet, scan the numbers on her red-inked P&L and ask a couple of key questions about her business' prior years and her personal finances.

"Helen (not her real name)," I said, "I'm sorry to have to be the one to tell you this, but your business is bankrupt." Pausing, with downcast eyes, I concluded, "And so are you."

Several months later, I received a similar call, this time from a husband-and-wife business. Same chorus, different verse. Once again, the trusty and venerable balance sheet told the sordid tale. The problem had been brewing for five years or more. And once more, good old Jim, rapidly turning into the Grim Reaper of Small Business, was called on to be the purveyor of bad news.

From those two incidents grew the idea to write this book.

For starters, such business-failure scenarios are definitely not fun for me or for my, uh, "customer." (In such cases, I volunteer my services.) More importantly however, the events that result from these situations are devastating to the party of the second part. Not only are the economic lives of the owners ruined, in the case of the husband-and-wife business, 40 employees also lost their jobs. How sad. How wasteful. And, in this case and so many others, how preventable.

From there grew the motivation to write this book.

In both cases, had the business owners asked for help from their CPA; had they talked to a lender or credit officer at their local bank (unfortunately, both businesses had been financed by the owners' 401(k)s, thus no business loans were involved); or had the business owners asked for professional help from me, from their local Small Business Development Center, or from any other Tom, Dick or Mary who knew how to read financial statements, these situations could have been turned around.

More to the point, had these business owners known how to understand and use financial statements on their own, these tragic events never would have happened in the first place.

There oughta be a law stipulating that you cannot start a business without first understanding, and learning, how to use your financial statements. You as well as every other small business owner should, before you're allowed to ring up your very first sale, be required to attend good old FSU (Financial Statement University); take a Financial Statement 101 class at your local SBDC or community college; find a financial statement mentor; or consult a guru. You should be required to do something!

From there grew the motivation to publish this book.

Digest its contents with care. After all, these are your life's savings you're talking about.

Chapter 1
What Sets Small Businesses Apart

"Once you make the commitment to start your own cabinet business, you are no longer a cabinet maker who happens to own a business. You are a business owner who happens to make cabinets."

Let me guess. I'll bet you believe, I mean truly believe, that your business builds the finest, let's say, cabinets in your community. Maybe in your state. Perhaps even in the entire USA.

Congratulations. That's nice. Yes, very nice. Great cabinets are essential to everyone and thus to the overall American economy. Why? Because if we don't have workable cabinets, then we can't get our socks out of the drawer in the morning and thus we'll be late to work whereupon our Gross National Product will plummet and the United States economy just might hit the skids. So congratulations on your contribution to our nation's financial well-being. Your great cabinets certainly play a role.

But while your great cabinets may have a positive effect on the Gross National Product, they won't necessarily have a positive effect on your business. You can make great cabinets until the cows come home, but if you don't shovel in more dollars than you shell out, your days of making great cabinets will be numbered.

Speaking of great products, you can't tell me for one minute that Mrs. Fields makes the tastiest chocolate chip cookies in the U.S. of A. No way! My grandmother, God rest her farmer's-wife soul, could make Mrs. Fields look like Tom Thumb when it comes to baking yummy chocolate chip cookies. I'd be willing to bet that so can a few hundred other grandmas around the country.

What Mrs. Fields *can* do better than my grandmother and all the other grandmas in the world is to make a tasty chocolate cookie *and* run a great business. That's what sets Mrs. Fields apart. And that's what will set you apart, too. Run a great business and you won't need to make great cabinets. But kick in great cabinets along with that great business and now what do you have? Why, you've got the next Microsoft, or Walmart, or Mrs. Field's Cookies, or whatever you want your business to look like when it grows up.

And what is the #1 determinant for running a great business? That's easy, assuming, of course, that you can find the capital required to start your business in the first place. The #1 determinant of your success will be the way you manage the fundamentals of your business' finances, which just happens to be the #1 shortcoming of most entrepreneurs and small business owners. Let's face it, who wants to learn about debits, and credits, and balance sheets, and profit and loss statements when there are cabinets to be made and customers to be satisfied and employees to be trained?

The Difference Between a Hero and a Successful Hero

So, Mr. or Mrs. Small Business Owner, whether you're starting a new business or managing an existing one, congratulations on your contribution to the American economy and thanks for the jobs you provide, the mouths you feed, and the services your customers enjoy. You are, in my humble opinion anyway, one of the economic heroes of this country in a time when heroes of any sort are in short supply.

But remember, if you want to be not only an economic hero, but more importantly, a *successful* economic hero, never lose sight of the fact that building cabinets is only a part of what you do. Furthermore, it's really not the most important part. Yes, you heard it here. Once you make the commitment to start your own cabinet business, you are no longer a cabinet maker who happens to own a business. You are a business owner who happens to make cabinets. There's a huge difference between the two, and it boils down to beans, beans, beans (as in dollars).

Don't worry, I don't expect you to actually become a bean counter yourself in order to build your successful business. Fortunately, your community has plenty of trained accountants for hire. So let's take a look at who they are and what they can do, along with what their role should be in your business. It isn't always what you might think.

Chapter 2
Your Accountant—Much, Much More
Than a Tax Preparer

"No one can give you conclusive advice on how to manage your business without that person first knowing how to understand, and use, your financial statements."

Before we go any further, you must first recognize one immutable fact about this small business career field you have chosen. It is, without a doubt, the loneliest career field of them all. Corporations, non-profit organizations, public entities and governments all have some kind of internal mentoring, consulting and/or training program established to provide guidance and direction for both their new and veteran managers and employees. Not so for us small business folks. We've embarked on this rollercoaster ride alone. When a problem rears its ugly head, too many of us choose to solve it ourselves, using the same trusty management tool our entrepreneurial predecessors have relied on for years—good old-fashioned trial-and-error.

Yes, love our small business as we may, this career field is a solo operation in which it's all too easy to lose our sense of perspective. As a result, we must constantly be on the lookout for help, especially when confronted with challenges. This much I can assure you:

technology aside, there is little that's new in the world of small business. Every new problem we face is really only a variation of a problem that has been around for years.

Where is the best place to look for that someone to help us avoid our upcoming pitfalls? Enter your friendly accountant. For purposes of this book we'll call him your CPA, but he could also be a tax advisor (TA) or enrolled agent (EA).

That's why this chapter is all about CPAs. Come on now. I'm sure you're asking why I would choose such a subject to lead off a book on small business financial statements. After all, CPAs come at the tail end of the business cycle, after the books have been closed, after the fiscal year is finished. They take those year-end numbers that we entrepreneurs and business owners have so painfully collected, run them through their mind-numbing exercises, and then hand us a number that represents a sum that we owe the Feds and the State. Whereupon they smile, fork over an invoice for services rendered and wave a friendly goodbye until next year.

Well, maybe that's what *your* CPA is presently doing, but that isn't what he/she should be doing. After all, your CPA is in a unique position—he is most likely the only outsider close enough to your business and your financials to offer general consulting advice on the direction of your business. He is, as we speak, probably the only person in a position to be able to help you decipher your financial statements *and* have the expertise to provide you with meaningful direction.

Please understand this following point: No one can give you conclusive advice on how to manage your business without that person first knowing how to understand and use your financial statements. Financial statements are the first place any professional consultant or turnaround expert worth his salt goes when asked to help a struggling business. The financial statements—assuming, of course, that they are correct—always tell the tale and your CPA is in a key position to interpret that tale.

And what if those financial statements aren't correct? Then this situation tells a tale of its own, and not a happy tale at that. As a rule, sloppy and erroneous financial statements portend a tale of mismanagement and lack of attention to detail, both of which are a precursor to failure.

Who Is Your CPA and What Should You Expect from Him?

You say your current CPA doesn't do this kind of general business consulting? Are you sure? Have you asked? Remember, this is your money and your future that's on the line, so you have good reason to inquire. After all, your CPA probably believes that you are like too many other independent-to-a-fault small business owners that he does business with and that you don't want help from anyone. Sure, in a perfect world, your CPA would volunteer to give you the advice you need to steer your business. Unfortunately, this isn't a perfect world. Recognize this fact and work around it. Ask for his help.

You say you'd welcome help from your CPA, but he isn't capable of providing the quality consulting help you need? Then you're definitely working with the wrong CPA. I can guarantee you this: there are a number of CPAs in or around your community who are capable of providing the kind of help you need; you simply haven't tried hard enough to find them. Ask the right questions (I'll get into that in a bit) and elevate your expectations to where they belong. You don't settle for mediocre quality when hiring employees do you? So why should hiring a CPA be any different?

Okay, so I'll admit that most CPAs, even the good ones, don't know diddly squat about the ins and outs of the cabinet business. But the good ones do know diddly squat about the ins and outs of interpreting all those numbers on your financial statements, and they do know diddly squat about entering all those numbers on your cash flow projections, and they do know diddly squat about managing receivables and managing inventory and generating financial statements on time. You see, they have long since learned that small business problems are generic, and they've been looking at these exact issues for their other small business clients for as many years as they've been counting their beans.

That's right. You're not the only small business in your CPA's portfolio. As a result, most CPAs have access to the financial statements of a number of other small business clients. Who knows, he might just have another cabinet maker as a client. Or at least another wood fabricator. Or certainly another light manufacturer. Thus, he'll have a number of like-minded figures to compare to your figures, without, of course, telling you from where they came.

Once you begin looking for the perfect CPA (some tips on how to go about this process are coming up shortly), you'll find that not all CPAs want to do the kind of consulting work I'm talking about here. Some simply want to do their number-crunching compliance work, so they're content to crank out your taxes and fill out any related forms. Which is fine. It's their business and they can run it any way they see fit. But these folks are not intended to be the service provider of choice for the savvy, successful small business owner or entrepreneur. Sorry, but savvy, successful entrepreneurs need meaning behind the numbers their CPAs provide.

Tips on How to Find the Best CPA for You

1. When selecting a CPA, you'll do best to consider one from a small-to medium-sized firm. These folks manage, or are involved in, small businesses, so they can better relate to your business. Plus, their fees don't have to finance marble foyers and gurgling waterfalls.

2. Develop a short list of candidates. Talk to other small business owners, your banker, your attorney or your insurance agent. The marketplace usually knows.

3. Interview your CPA candidates as if you were interviewing a prospective employee for a key position. Most will generally allot you 30 free minutes to do so. (Remember, they have but one product to sell: their time. Learn to respect it!)

4. Ask the following questions of your CPA candidates:

- How long have you been a CPA? What other licenses do you hold?
- Do you have any client businesses similar to mine?
- Who will actually be doing my work?
- What are your billing rates? How are your fees calculated?
- What can I do to keep my billings to a minimum?
- Do you provide consulting advice? Have you done so for others? Can I contact several of them for a referral? Do you have any established consulting programs in place?
- If I were to ask for an annual checkup on my business, what are some of the subjects you would review?
- Might I need to upgrade my present accounting system? If so, describe the procedure, the product and the approximate cost.

5. When interviewing candidates, ask for a list of current clients you can contact. Then check those references, just as you would the references of a potential employee.

6. Once you've narrowed your list to two or three candidates, indulge in a breakfast or lunch with your top picks. Besides getting a free lunch (if they don't pick up the tab you've learned a valuable lesson already), you'll get an idea of the synergy that could develop between the two of you. Synergy is always a necessary element of any successful tax advisor/client relationship.

When to Use Your CPA

Once you've located and retained the CPA of your dreams, there are at least two times a year that you absolutely, positively must meet with him and a third time that's optional:

Session #1 – Tax Planning and Strategizing: The two of you should meet in October or early November if you are on a January 1 to December 31 fiscal year; otherwise one or two months before your fiscal year ends. This meeting will be the time to review your year-to-date financial statements, estimate your year-end results and make your year-end tax plans. Don't wait until December—do it while you still will have plenty of time to make the moves he'll suggest.

Session #2 – Annual Checkup and Physical: Just as you should ask your doctor for a physical checkup every year, you need to do the same for your business—it has its aches and pains too. Don't wait until March or April when the financial news is stale. Schedule this session as soon as you've generated your year-end financial statements. Ask your CPA to review your year-end financials, both

P&L and balance sheet. Also, have him review your business' key indicators (we'll talk about those in Chapter 8). What is the good news, what is the bad? How is the business trending compared to the previous year? What danger signals does he see on the horizon?

Assuming your CPA charges $150 per hour, these first two visits will cost you upwards of $300. A small price to pay for such a large potential reward.

While accountants are usually the best of the outsider options for providing advice on running your business, they are not the only option. Bankers, as you are about to see, can also play a similar role.

Chapter 3
Your Banker's #1 Service
Is Not Providing Money

"The #1 service your banker provides is to hold you accountable."

Let's begin this chapter with a question. Paper out. Pencils ready.

"What is the #1 service your banker provides?"

Finished? Let me guess what you've concluded. I'll guess your answer had something to do with cash or loans or money, right? Perhaps you said "provides capital." Or "makes loans." Or maybe "gives away cash to needy entrepreneurs." Am I right? Was that your answer?

Sorry, but that wouldn't be my answer. My answer would be: "The #1 service your banker provides is to hold you accountable." Yep, that's my answer and I'm sticking to it. Accountability it is.

Let's face it, most of us entered this small business career field because we were drawn to the independence it offers. We liked the freedom, the lack of structure. We tried making a living the other way and were crummy employees; we had all the answers and our bosses didn't. And so, we moved on to a vocation where we could do things our way and not someone else's. We made the decision to start our own business.

That's the American way of doing things and, in my opinion, such freedom and independence is worth all of the related downsides. However, one of those downsides is that we end up with no boss of our own, and thus no accountability. And while we think that's nirvana (and in many ways, it is), in one way it isn't. That's because accountability, in the right hands, is good for the soul, as well as for the business.

The message here? Everyone in our vocation should be accountable to someone.

Accountability? What's the Big Deal?

Every successful business owner needs a goal to pursue, whether that goal is publicly stated or not. And being the less-than-perfect individuals that we are, we need someone to congratulate us when we accomplish our goal and someone to chastise us when we don't. Enter our friendly bankers. They are the only ones who can get away with the chastising part. Our employees can't, and our vendors can't. Our spouse probably could, but he/she doesn't understand the extent of whatever it is we have gotten ourselves into. Yes, we need accountability in our business life and our banker is, in most cases, the only person in a position to apply it.

You'd better believe that bankers, the good ones anyway, will wield accountability like a razor-edged sword once they've made the decision to dole out their cash. They'll ask you the tough questions and demand accurate answers, and they'll do many of the things that a boss or a board of directors would otherwise do. After all, they too are a significant investor in your business. Thus, they have the right to hold you accountable since they've long ago learned that accountability is good. So lighten up when your banker tells you that you need to improve your current ratio. He's doing it for your own good as well as for his.

Not too long ago, I worked with a local business owner who had one of the most anemic balance sheets you can imagine. The right side was teeming with unpaid liabilities, including a mid-six-figure loan from a local bank and a dozen or so VISA cards that had long since been maxed out. The harried owner was paying more each year in interest charges than he was taking home.

When I asked him what his banker had to say about his long list of high-interest liabilities, he sheepishly told me that the banker wasn't aware of them. The business owner had had the same banker for three years, and he had never been asked to explain the details of his balance sheet, including his imposing inventory of debts. As long as the interest payments kept coming, the banker was asking no questions.

This banker was doing the owner no favors. To the contrary, the owner was being let off the hook. By the time I was brought in, the situation had gone too far, for too long. The business was on its last leg, the banker was embarrassed, and the owner was burned out.

Impressing Your Banker

Okay, so once you've found a banker who will hold you accountable and, at the same time, lend you the money you need, you will want to impress him. Here are several suggestions on how you can accomplish just that:

1. Prepare a three-year pro-forma (projected P&L and balance sheet). Keep it current, updating the actual results. Meanwhile, keep your bankers updated on your progress. They'll know you understand financials, they'll know you understand spreadsheets, and most of all, they'll know you get it. (Can't handle the technology involved in that information-gathering exercise? Then have your CPA or bookkeeper teach you. Or, have him/her do it.)

2. Call your banker more often than he calls you. Call him with the good news, and call him with the bad. Bankers don't like surprises, especially those of the negative variety.

3. Follow your banker's suggestions. Most good bankers keep notes on their meetings; they know when you haven't followed up.

4. Invite your banker to visit your business at least once a year. Let him kick your tires. Don't wait for him to request a visit, beat him to the punch.

5. Face up to the fact that in the early stages of your business, you'll have to personally guarantee your loans. Bankers aren't making an exception when they require this of you. That's just the way they conduct their business. You'd ask for guarantees too if you were in their shoes.

6. Don't expect your banker to be a venture capitalist— excessive risk isn't in his vocabulary. Banks need collateral, they need personal guarantees and they, in most cases, don't fund start-ups.

Finally, one more key point about bankers. They know more than you think they do about running a successful business. Okay, so they don't own a business themselves. That decision usually has to do with their stomach for accepting risk, not their knowledge base. Most lending officers, the folks you and I deal with when we want their cash, have a large portfolio of businesses they service. They know when our gross margin isn't what it should be and they know when our payroll is higher than it should be. They know how to read, and understand, and interpret the minutiae of our financial statements, often better than we do.

Don't lose sight of the fact that while I'm encouraging you to ask for help from accountants and bankers, I'm not letting you off the hook when it comes to understanding the numbers your business generates. While those professional outsiders can certainly help, the best scenario is having a basic understanding of financial statements and then calling in the outsiders.

That leads us to Chapter 4. It's now time to set the wheels in motion and generate an understanding about how to use your financial statements to help you manage your business.

Chapter 4
Use Your Financial Statements
to Manage Your Business

"Financial statements can tell you what you did yesterday (profit and loss statements), where you are today (balance sheets), and where you'll be tomorrow (cash flow projections and budgets)."

While this is a business book designed to help you use financial statements to manage your business, business is not the only place that utilizing financial statements can come in handy. Let's suppose, just for a moment, that you're at home and it's the end of the month. It's, argghh, bill-paying time again. You gulp down two aspirin, crack open a beer and pull out the monthly stack of bills, all $4,000 of them. Then you peek in your checkbook and the sad little number in the right-hand column totals exactly half of that $4,000. You now know you have a cash flow problem.

Now let's suppose that instead of beating the desk, tearing your hair and cursing the IRS like you normally do, you phone a financial advisor and ask for help. Here's what the financial advisor will do when he arrives on the scene:

Step #1: He'll add up your bills and subtract your checkbook balance, just like you did. Eureka, he's created a cash flow statement and determined that you do, in fact, have a cash flow problem.

Step #2: Next he'll ask what bills you're going to have in the upcoming month. The same as last month? Will there be anything new? Then he'll inquire about the income you expect to receive during that period. The same as last month? Will there be anything new? Whereupon he'll subtract your anticipated bills from your anticipated income and determine approximately where you'll be, cash flow-wise, one month from now. Eureka, he's created cash flow projections.

Step #3: Now that he understands the depth of your problem—both today and tomorrow—he'll question you about what you've done to get to this sorry point. Then, after you've shrugged your shoulders and scratched your head and mumbled "I dunno", he'll pull out your checkbook, your VISA statement and your bank statement, and begin categorizing your monthly expenses. After he's categorized those recurring expenses—mortgage, utilities, insurance, healthcare, entertainment, etc.—he'll review your income (aka revenue) from the past month. Once he's finished tabulating your income and has subtracted your expenses, he'll have a piece of paper that points out exactly how many bucks you took in last month as opposed to how many you shelled out. Eureka, he's created a profit and loss statement.

Step #4: Now that Mr. Financial Advisor knows the depth of your problem and now that he knows why the problem occurred, he's ready to find a solution. To find that solution, he will need to know what outside resources you have that will allow you to generate the cash you'll need in order to settle your bills. After asking the right questions, he'll have a tidy little worksheet that will list all the assets you own, including those that can be readily turned into cash (current assets) and those that can't (fixed assets). On the other side of his tidy little worksheet, he'll list any liabilities, i.e., debts you have, such as outstanding bills, car payments and mortgages. Then, assuming your assets total more than your liabilities, he'll determine your net worth. Eureka, he's created a balance sheet.

Now, at last, Mr. Financial Adviser understands the depth of your problem (you owe $2,000), he knows the cause of your problem (you lost $2,500 on the slots in Las Vegas), he knows the solution to your immediate problem (you'll need to cash in a CD) and he knows the long-term solution to your problem (either no more Las Vegas jaunts, negotiate a hefty raise or find a night job).

We're Talking Business 101 Here

There you have it. I've just given you a quick overview of Home Business 101, which also works the same way when it comes to Small Business 101. This example illustrates exactly why you need financial statements. Financial statements tell you what you did yesterday (profit and loss statements), where you are today (balance sheets) and where you're going to be tomorrow (cash flow projections and budgets).

Using Your Financials to Manage Your Business

A wise, old sage once stated, *"If you can't measure it, you can't manage it."* Well, whoever that wise old sage was, he/she was definitely right. Management (of your financial resources) is what financial statements are all about. Thus, financials measure what you've done so that you can learn how to manage what you do, be that at your home or at your business.

You say you aren't using them? Then you're wasting money. And you aren't alone. I know of a company with $3 million in sales that employs a $50,000-a-year controller and a $30,000-a-year accounts receivable and accounts payable person. Tack on another $10,000 or so for miscellaneous accounting-related expenses (computer, software, supplies, employee benefits, etc.) and we're talking $90,000 a year to, among other things, generate financial statements. So what kind of business decision is it to shell out $90,000 a year to generate data that you don't use?

One additional point about financial statements: I can tell within minutes of looking at a business' financial statements, what the owner's personal strengths and weaknesses are. I can tell whether the owner is neat and orderly—his financial statements will be up to date and his numbers will be in sync. I can tell whether or not he has a spending problem—a review of his expenses will provide that information. I can tell whether or not he has a follow-up problem—the status of his accounts receivable will tell that story. I can tell whether or not he has an attention-to-detail problem—the size of his inventory will be the tattletale. I can tell whether or not he has a problem managing employees—his payroll as a percentage of his sales will be the key indicator here. I can tell whether or not he has a partying problem—the entertainment expense account tells no lies. It's a fact, a business owner's financial statements are better than any inkblot test or personality profile when it comes to getting inside a business owner's head.

Keeping Score

One final point on financial statements in particular and numbers in general. While I know that the collection of data, and the numbers that go along with it, conjures visions of green eye-shades, musty ledgers and dimly lit rooms to many of us, nothing could be further from the truth. After all, numbers are nothing more than records of activities, activities that come as the result of things you and I do.

Just as the Yankee Stadium scoreboard displays the number of baseball players that have crossed home plate, so it is with your scoreboard—your P&L, balance sheet and cash flow projections. Sell a cabinet and that activity turns into a number on the P&L. Buy a lathe and the cost turns into a number on the balance sheet. Purchase a box of cigars for the guy who buys your cabinets and that figure shows up on your P&L.

In short, every number has a home.

Now that we're agreed that financial statements are a key element of running a business, let's discuss my favorite statement of them all: the balance sheet. Okay, I'll admit it, I love a good balance sheet and I hate a bad one, and it takes me less than 60 seconds to tell the difference between the two.

Chapter 5
Understand Your Balance Sheet –
The Most Telltale Financial Statement of Them All

"The balance sheet doesn't care a whit about if only. *It only cares about* what is. *"*

The balance sheet is the most important financial statement of them all. While the P&L provides a vehicle by which to improve operations, the balance sheet (sometimes called a statement of financial position) is a state-of-the-union scorecard. A balance sheet gives you a grade of how healthy your business is. Or isn't.

Years ago, I watched along with the rest of the business world, as a Fortune 500 company, Enron, slid down the financial tubes, thanks to crooked management and financial systems that went awry. Every day it seemed that fresh tales of management and financial abuse came to light. The slant on Enron's failure that's of interest to us small business owners is this: a well-respected analyst had been loudly touting Enron stock in advance of its decline, focusing, as stock touts are prone to do, on the *future potential* of the company. The tout overlooked, however, the real issue: Enron didn't have a strong enough balance sheet to survive the following week, let alone enjoy its *future potential.* In other words, Enron couldn't even pay its bills.

The moral of the story:

Tomorrows can never come if the business can't get past today.

This adage applies to Mom's Diner as well as to Enron. If I've heard these laments once from small business owners, I've heard them a gazillion times:

- "If only I could start over again."
- "If only I could catch up on my bills."
- "If only I could get the bank loan paid off."

Sorry, but *if only* doesn't count in the world of business. The balance sheet doesn't care a whit about *if only*. It only cares about *what is*.

As mentioned before, the balance sheet is the first place to look to determine the health of a business. It's a snapshot of a company's financial position at that particular point in time. You can crank out a balance sheet every day if you choose, and it has immediate relevance. It measures the business' overall financial health today, right now, at this very instant. It shows what the business owns—its assets; it shows what the business owes—its liabilities; and it shows what's left over after subtracting what's owed from what's owned— the business' net worth.

Let's take a look at a sample balance sheet and see how it works.

Rubber Ducky Inc.
Balance Sheet as Of Dec. 31, 2002

Current Assets:	Current Year	Prior Year
Cash	$25,000	$20,000
Accounts Receivable	100,000	80,000
Inventory	125,000	75,000
Total Current Assets	$250,000	$175,000
Fixed Assets:		
Furniture & Fixtures	50,000	45,000
Equipment	150,000	125,000
Total Fixed Assets	200,000	170,000
TOTAL ASSETS	**$450,000**	**$345,000**
Current Liabilities		
Accounts Payable	75,000	70,000
VISA Payable	25,000	20,000
Total Current Liabilities	100,000	90,000
Long Term Liabilities		
Uncle Charley Note Payable	150,000	160,000
President's Note Payable	50,000	50,000
Total Long Term Liabilities	200,000	210,000
TOTAL LIABILITIES	300,000	300,000
Net Worth	150,000	45,000
Total Liabilities and Net Worth	**$450,000**	**$345,000**

Taking a Physical of Your Business

So here's your balance sheet exercise for today. Let's pretend you asked for my advice on the health of your company. We're talking taking a physical here, not an autopsy.

So haul out your business' balance sheet and let's wade through the following exercises together. Let's review some of the key figures and develop several key ratios and indicators from those figures. You'll need your balance sheet from a year ago, and your most recent profit and loss statement. We'll use the Rubber Ducky balance sheet as an example to help us understand how the numbers shake out.

We will, incidentally, discuss in more detail the use and application of ratios and percentages when we get into explaining how to develop a key indicator report. Suffice it to say that ratios and percentages provide a tool by which to measure the relationships between the numbers your business generates, allowing you to compare them to previous numbers, as well as to numbers that similar businesses generate.

One more thing before we get started. I'm assuming that your accounting system is generating accurate and trustworthy numbers. If it isn't, we have a much bigger problem.

• **Exercise #1 – Current Ratio Computation:** Let's first compute your current ratio (a ratio that measures your business' liquidity) by dividing current assets by current liabilities on your balance sheet. For your information, this is the first place the bankers look. What's happening here is that they are determining the liquidity of your business. If you have more current assets (assets that can be turned into cash within 30 days) than current liabilities (debts that must be paid within 30 days), you can cover any 30-day calls on your cash that might occur. If the resulting ratio is, say, 2-to-1 or higher (current assets over current liabilities), most bankers would consider you to have a healthy current ratio and thereby to be financially healthy. If the ratio is in the neighborhood of 1-to-1, then you are perched on the perimeter of your danger zone. If, however, the current ratio is less than 1-to-1, it's time to hitch up your pants.

Using Rubber Ducky's balance sheet as an example, you can see that its current ratio is a healthy 2.5-to-1 ($250,000 divided by $100,000). Another positive note for the Rubber Ducky business is trend. Its current ratio last year was 1.94-to-1 ($175,000 divided by $90,000). This year that ratio has improved.

After completing this exercise, in addition to your business' general health, I'll know how immediate any cash flow problem you have may be. I'll also have a good idea as to how much time you'll have to solve your problems.

• **Exercise #2 – Debt-to-Equity Review:** This is the ratio of what you owe (debt)-to-(equity)what you own. In other words, if your equity (aka your net worth) is more than you owe, then your debt-equity ratio will be less than 1-to-1. This quick exercise gives the reader a snapshot view of who it is that can legally call the shots in your business—the bank, the creditors or you.

As you can see from Rubber Ducky's balance sheet, its debt-equity ratio is 2-to-1; the $300,000 in liabilities divided by the $150,000 in net worth (equity). We're seeing a nice trend here as well: the prior year's debt-equity ratio was 6.6-to-1 ($300,000 divided by $45,000).

After completing this exercise, I will know who really is the majority owner of your business. Is it you, your bank or your creditors? In Rubber Ducky's case, the creditors own more of the company than the owner does. Eventually, as the company matures, this should change.

• **Exercise #3 – Accounts Receivable Review:** Your accounts receivable are (unless you are running a cash business and you don't have any receivables) an integral part of your current assets. Accounts receivable represents, in effect, cash-in-waiting, which means they are the next best thing to cash.

First, I need to know if your accounts receivable are, in fact, collectable, and I need to know how quickly your customers typically pay. I'll look at your P&L to determine the dollar amount of last month's sales. Now, I'll look at the accounts receivable balance on the balance sheet. Are the two numbers in the same ballpark? If, for instance, your receivables are $200,000 and your monthly sales are $100,000, this tells me you probably have a collection problem. You've got two months of sales in your receivables which means that either your customers are paying in 60 days (too slow!), or you have some extremely slow payers in your customer mix. Or worse, you have a festering lump of ancient receivables that aren't going to be collected at all. Which means, if you will be forced to write off a portion of those receivables, you'll adversely affect your current ratio. A quick look at your accounts receivable aging—an updated list of all those folks who owe you money including the age of their invoices—will tell the ultimate tale.

After completing this exercise, I will now have an idea of the relative collectability of your receivables and of the health and well-being of your current ratio. I will also have an idea of how well your office and its systems and controls are being managed. Good office systems and dependable controls usually result in collectable accounts receivable.

• **Exercise #4 – Inventory Review:** Another key element of your balance sheet (unless you're a service provider and don't carry inventory for sale or resale) is inventory. Since inventory, similar to accounts receivable, is a current asset, it's an important element of the current ratio computation as well. I'll look at your monthly sales figure from your P&L and compare that to the dollar amount of your inventory in order to determine whether the business has too much or too little inventory.

This is a more difficult exercise than the accounts receivable exercise, because the balance sheet shows inventory at cost while the sales figure from the P&L includes the addition of profit (hopefully there's plenty of it) and any cost of goods sold that you might have. I've got to make a quick mental calculation to adjust the inventory figure on your balance sheet to include that profit and cost of goods sold figure. Once I've made that mental calculation, I'll be able to estimate approximately how many months' sales you have in inventory and how many times a year you're turning your inventory.

Let's say you have $100,000 in sales and $200,000 in inventory. Upon asking the right questions, I'll determine that you mark up your inventory by, say, 100 percent to include profit and cost of goods sold. Thus, that inventory, when converted to sales dollars, is really $400,000, which means that you have four months of sales in your inventory. This also means, you're turning your inventory three times a year.

In essence, an inventory turn of 10 or more means you're turning your inventory almost once a month. A turn of six means you're turning it every two months. A turn of two indicates twice a year. Are these turns good or bad, you ask? Well, you'd have to consult your industry trade associations for that answer. Your CPA may help you answer this question too.

Once I've completed this exercise, I'll have an idea of how well your business manages its inventory compared to other businesses in your industry. I'll know approximately how many times your inventory turns. Or translated, I'll know how well you understand the role of inventory (after all, it's a very dangerous form of cash) and how well you manage it. I'll also have a good idea as to how well you manage details, since inventory is one of the most important details of them all.

• **Exercise #5 – Liability Review:** Next, I'll review your accounts payable aging (similar to your accounts receivable aging, this report details your creditors and the age of the monies due them), your notes payable and any outside liabilities that you might have. If you were the Rubber Ducky owner, I'd ask you about that note to Uncle Charley. Do you really have to pay it back? If so, when? What is the interest rate? What is Charley's collateral? How about that note to yourself (president's note payable); do you need to pay that back anytime soon?

I'll also look to see if you are financing your business with credit cards. If you are, this will tell me something about your credit rating, something about your interest expense and something about your ability to find money elsewhere. While I'm aware that many start-ups use credit card debt to finance their early growth, if your company is more than two years old and you're still using credit card debt to pay your bills, then something is amiss. We'll need to explore alternatives.

Once I've completed this exercise, I'll have a strong indication of:

- Your credit rating and how easy, or difficult, it is for you to find money.

- How well you manage your relationships with vendors and creditors.
- How you are perceived by the credit community.

• **Exercise #6 – Comparison to Prior Year:** First, there is one rule that must be remembered whenever you're dealing with numbers. Numbers are always the most useful when compared to other numbers. With that overriding rule in mind, it's now time to dig out your balance sheet from one year ago. We need to know not only where *you are,* but also where *you've been.*

Imagine, for instance, that today your current ratio is, say, 1.2-to-1. Is that good or is it bad? My response would be that it's good if a year ago, it was .8-to-1. On the other hand, it's bad if, a year ago, it was 2-to-1. It's trend that counts, which is why we need yesterday's numbers to answer the *good or bad* question.

Look at Rubber Ducky's current ratio compared to the prior year. This is definitely a figure that's trending in the right direction. Ditto with its debt-equity ratio. The only disturbing trend I can see on the Rubber Ducky balance sheet is its inventory, which increased by 66 percent over the prior year (from $75,000 to $125,000). I'd need some answers as to why the big upsurge.

Back to Your Business

Okay, so are your receivables leaner, i.e., has your percent over 60 days gone down this year compared to a year ago? Is your inventory leaner? Is your credit card debt up or down? How about your liabilities as a whole? And, of course, your net worth, where is it compared to a year ago? In order to answer these questions and more, you can understand why it's necessary to dust off yesterday's balance sheet and compare the numbers.

While on the subject of comparing numbers, here's a tip that you should adopt the day you design the format for your first financial statement. Always include at least two columns of numbers on your P&L and balance sheet and preferably three. The first column should be current year, the second column should be prior year, and the third column, assuming that you prepare an annual budget, should include your budgeted numbers. Using this multi-columnar format, you'll always have at least one and sometimes two numbers to use for comparison purposes.

Once you've concluded the exercise of comparing today's numbers to yesterday's numbers, you'll know officially where your company's financial condition—and your business as a whole—is trending. Is it trending up or trending down?

Having determined the state of your business' financial solvency, it's time to take a look at what it is that's determining its trend. What's causing it to trend up, trend down or hold steady, and what changes do you need to make to change any negative trends? This story will be told by your profit and loss statement.

Chapter 6
Use Your Profit and Loss Statement to Manage Your Business' Direction

"There are only three options when you want to positively impact your profitability: 1) decrease expenses, 2) increase gross margin or 3) increase sales."

While the balance sheet is a difficult financial statement to read, the profit and loss statement is, at first glance anyway, more easily understandable. Heck, you start at the top of the statement with your sales (or revenues), then, working down, you subtract whatever those sales cost (cost of goods sold) are. Then subtract all the other expenses that aren't directly related to your products or services (overhead), and what's left over is profitability. How linear, wouldn't you say? How easy. How quick.

Sadly, because of this top-to-bottom effect, most entrepreneurs feel they are capable of reading a profit and loss statement and thus are inclined to believe that they understand it. They get lured into this complacency by the relative simplicity and ease of starting at the top and working their way down. But reading a P&L is one thing, understanding it is another, and using it as a tool to manage the business is yet another.

While it's true that the P&L is a relatively easy statement to read, it's not until you begin using the P&L to actually manage the direction of your business that you will really learn to understand what it is and what it isn't. It's not a document to be used only to determine your bottom-line profitability and then pay your taxes. It's a document to be used to manage the direction of your business.

A Word about Format and Selecting Key Percentages

Before we get into using the profit and loss statement as a management tool, let's go back to the topic of format for a minute, as discussed in the previous chapter. In addition to the prior year and budget columns, the P&L requires still another column entitled *percent of sales*. This column will appear to the right of each of the year-to-date, prior year and budget columns, and will allow the reader to quickly determine what percentage of the total sales each line item constitutes. Sure, the page now becomes much busier and harder to read, but remember we're looking to create a management tool here, not a children's book.

Let's take a look at what an abbreviated profit and loss statement might look like for a small manufacturing company:

Rubber Ducky Inc.
Profit and Loss Statement for
the Year Ending Dec. 31, 2002

	Current Year	% Sales	Prior Year	% Sales
Sales	$1,000,000	100	$800,000	100
Cost of Goods Sold				
Raw Materials	125,000	12.5	95,000	11.9
Direct Labor (Salaries)	350,000	35	300,000	37.5
Cost of Goods Sold	475,000	47.5	395,000	49.4
Gross Profit	525,000	52.5	405,000	50.6
General & Administrative Expenses				
Depreciation	25,000	2.5	20,000	2.5
Rent	75,000	7.5	75,000	9.4
Office & Admin. Salaries	150,000	15	125,000	15.6
All that Other Stuff	125,000	12.5	110,000	13.8
Total Expenses	375,000	37.5	330,000	41.3
Pre-Tax Profit	$150,000	15	$75,000	9.4

While every number and percentage on the P&L will have meaning, there are several that are more important than others. Those key numbers and percentages include:

- **Profitability Compared to Prior Year:** Rubber Ducky earned $150,000 in pre-tax dollars this year, compared to $75,000 the prior year. In terms of real dollars, this is certainly a meaningful increase, wouldn't you agree?

  More importantly however, Rubber Ducky returned 15 percent on sales this year ($150,000 profit on sales of $1,000,000) compared to 9.4 percent the prior year, another solid increase. Incidentally, this means that for every dollar the company sold, it made 15 cents in pre-tax profit, as compared to 9.4 cents the year before.

  We've discovered a reassuring trend with this example: Rubber Ducky's profitability is increasing, both in real dollars and as a percentage of sales. Now, check out your P&L from last year and then this year; can the same be said of your business?

- **Gross Margin:** Gross margin (GM) is the percentage of profit you've made on sales *after* deducting the cost of goods sold, but *before* deducting your general and administrative expenses. Hence the term *gross* margin.

  To be able to understand the relevancy of the gross margin percentage, every business owner should know exactly what the industry gross margin standard is for the product or service he is providing. For instance, I recently worked with a light manufacturing company reporting a gross margin of 22 percent. Meanwhile, after checking with the fellow's trade association, we learned that the industry standard was 37 percent. Since the sales of this company were $2,000,000 at the time, this owner was giving away 15 percentage points in the GM category (the difference between 22 percent and 37 percent), which amounts to $300,000 per year! How many small businesses can afford to leave that kind of money on the table?

If you're using your P&L simply to measure your profitability and to pay your taxes, then the pre-tax net profit figure at the bottom of the page will be the first and last place you will look. If, however, you're using the P&L to manage your business, then bottom line profitability will still be at the top of your list followed closely by gross margin. This is because it won't take you long to learn that the greatest opportunity to make significant changes in profitability usually lies in gross margin.

- **Overhead as a Percentage of Sales:** Overhead is represented by the total of all the general and administrative expenses, or in the case of Rubber Ducky, $375,000. Since this figure is 37.5 percent of sales, it represents Rubber Ducky's ability to manage its overhead expenses. In this case, the 37.5 percent figure shows an improving trend over the 41.2 percent figure from last year.

As your company grows, you, too, should be able to operate more efficiently, similar to Rubber Ducky. So the percentage of your total general and administrative expenses, as a percentage of sales, should decrease as your sales increase. If this isn't happening, contrary to what your increasing sales figures are telling you, you may not, in truth, be growing at all.

Many mature businesses will also divide their expenses into departments such as finance and administration, sales and marketing, operations/production, etc. Such divisions will allow you to determine, and compare to industry averages, the percentage of every sales dollar spent per department.

- **Salaries as a Percentage of Sales:** Salaries are usually the single largest individual line item on the P&L, whether they are those that are included in the cost-of-goods-sold section of the P&L or those under general and administrative expenses. You can quickly spot trends in the amount of salaries paid by comparing the percentages from one period to the next. In the Rubber Ducky example, both salary accounts are trending down, which means Rubber Ducky's management is doing an excellent job of managing that hugely important expense account.

- **Your Largest Expense Line Items as a Percentage of Sales:** After looking at the categories mentioned above, scan the individual line items within the general & administrative expense category to determine where the biggest numbers are hiding— and hence the biggest opportunities to make a difference. Then determine the trend of those line items by comparing percentages between the year to date and the prior year.

  You say your entertainment expense has risen from 2 percent to 2.8 percent of total sales? Better start sitting in the back of the plane. Telephone expenses up? How many cell phones have you handed out and what are they being used for? Utilities up? Who's responsible for setting the thermostat and turning off the lights at night?

Affecting the Direction of Your Business' Trend

Now that you understand the basics of how to read a P&L, it's time to give me a call again. That's me, your trusty, reliable and grossly-underpaid financial consultant. Let's see if we can positively influence your business' trend and, in the process, positively impact its profitability. So pull out your own P&L, complete with (at least) the prior year comparisons and with the percent of sales columns filled out.

Before we dive in, however, you must first understand one principle of profitability. There are only three ways for any business to increase its profitability: 1) decrease expenses, 2) increase gross margin or 3) increase sales.

• Step One: Decrease Expenses

When wanting to increase profitability, why should you head for expenses before zeroing in on gross margin or sales? Because while expenses may not have the potential to make the biggest change in the bottom line, they are the easiest of the three categories to impact. Ben Franklin was right—a penny saved *is*, in fact, a penny earned. Save $100 on your telephone bill and that $100 drops straight to the bottom line.

The bottom-line impact of cutting expenses is not the same as, say, adding $100 to your sales. Sure, adding $100 to sales is impactful, but just how impactful is it? Maybe you add 10 bucks to your profits (if you're earning 10 cents on the dollar), but then, maybe you don't. It all depends on what you're selling, how much you're marking up what you're selling, who pays the freight, whether you get paid on time, and, well, you get the point. Increased sales don't always lead to increased profits.

Don't make the mistake of overlooking expenses as the first place to go when you're set on changing your earning trend. Don't overlook expenses simply because there might be some conflict involved in making the necessary changes, i.e., cutting salaries, changing insurance providers or asking your vendors for discounts. Don't overlook expenses simply because it's a plodding and laborious exercise. And, don't overlook expenses simply because cutting expenses isn't as much fun as creating sales.

Now that you're digging into expenses, it's time to interject a word about budgeting. If you aren't budgeting, you should be, and if you are budgeting, you should consider zero-basing your budget. Zero-basing consists of first making the assumption that all your expenses are *zero* and then starting from that point and determining exactly what they should be. In order to determine what they should be, you need to take each line item and reconstruct it—ask three insurance agents for quotes; call FedEx instead of assuming UPS is your best option; call in the power company to do an audit on your electricity consumption.

Unfortunately, zero-basing is not what most small businesses do when budgeting expenses. They take the easy way out and simply tack on a logical inflation figure, say 3 percent, to last year's expenses. Your phone bill last year was $1,000? Then budget $1,030 this year and move on to the next line item. No fuss, no muss, no time wasted. And no opportunity for reducing your expenses.

Sure, zero-basing expenses takes more time than adding a flat percentage, but once you've zero-based the first time it will be much easier the following year. Then you'll have a template. You'll also learn how easy it can be to positively impact profitability. As a result, you just might find yourself zero-basing specific line-item expenses year-round. It can actually be fun if you set goals for yourself.

• Step Two: Increase Gross Margin

Gross margin can be positively impacted three ways: 1) by increasing your prices, 2) by lowering your cost of raw materials or 3) by increasing your production efficiency.

Pricing is always the easiest of the three to change. You say you think you'll sell 10,000 widgets this year at $4.50 each? Then bump the price a measly quarter to $4.75 and you'll drop another $2,500 to your bottom line. Simple, quick and usually quite easy, assuming, of course, that the market will bear the increase. You get the same kind of results here that you get by cutting expenses—the dollar amount of the price increase drops straight to the bottom line.

The second key element of gross margin is raw material cost. You'll need to review the prices you're paying your vendors to improve this figure and then follow up with negotiation. Is your company getting big enough to negotiate better prices from your vendors? You'll never know unless you ask. (Note: If you're a service provider you won't have raw materials to worry about.)

The third element of gross margin is production efficiency. You can measure this by studying your labor within the cost-of-goods-sold category as expressed as a percentage of sales. Has the percentage decreased in the last year? Then congratulations, you have become more efficient.

• Step Three: Increase Sales

At last, the fun part of increasing profitability—for most entrepreneurs anyway: Increasing sales.

Unfortunately, most entrepreneurs first turn to sales when times get tough. You say your business is losing money? The first impulse is to throw more sales at the problem. So, what happens? You add more sales to an already inefficient organization, your inefficiency increases, and you lose even *more* money.

The key point here? Getting the organization operating efficiently comes first. Once you have that under control, then it's time to add sales.

Sadly, most small business owners are hung up on sales. "How's business?" you ask another small business owner. "Fantastic," the fellow responds. After all, his sales were up 20 percent. *Wow*, you think. *He's one up on me; my sales were only up 15 percent.* Never mind that the guy lost 5 percent on every dollar he sold. You aren't about to hear about that.

Certainly, sales are more fun to pursue and a good juicy sale will always bring out the goose bumps in most small business owners. Plus, it simply feels really, really good when you land a big, juicy sale. However, it isn't sales that impact your bank account. It's bottom-line profitability that counts. No, wait. It's really cash in the checking account that counts, but we'll talk about that in Chapter 7. In the meantime, if you want to make it to the big time, get off the sales kick and onto the profitability kick. It's profitability that makes a successful business, not sales.

Still, once you have all your ducks in a row, you'll want to focus on bumping up sales.

The Role of Training

Okay, so exactly how do you go about increasing sales? Well it isn't always by adding more products, it isn't always by adding more sales people, and it isn't always by expanding territories. No, the best way to increase sales is by increasing sales *training*. That's right, by taking the resources you have now and making them better. Those resources include your sales staff and your customer service folks and, most of all, the people who manage them. In most small businesses, that person is probably the owner, and maybe the sales manager if your company is large enough to have one.

Please remember that sales is more skill than art. Most of us think of a sales person in terms of a list of predisposed personality traits, i.e., friendly, gregarious, good talker, goal driven, to name a few. If someone we interview possesses these outward traits, then she must be a salesperson. But before you hire someone who possesses those traits, remember that since sales is a skill, it can be honed and sharpened, and training is the best way to accomplish that. I'll take a trained professional salesperson any day over a gregarious, story-telling extrovert.

Unfortunately, most small business owners aren't chomping at the bit to funnel their hard-earned dollars into training. That's because we view training as an expense, not as the investment it really is.

A Word About Benchmarking

As we saw in the prior chapter about balance sheets, it's helpful to compare expenses—along with all the other numbers on your financial statements—to the figures of other businesses in your field. That's known as benchmarking. Webster defines the word *benchmark* as "a standard by which something can be measured or judged." Most trade associations have collected an array of benchmarked figures for every line item on your P&L. As a result, they have, in effect, created a standard business model for the industry.

Is your gross margin in line with industry standards? Are your general and administrative expenses too high? How about salaries as a percentage of sales? Compare your return on sales (ROS), sales per employee or entertainment as a percentage of sales. You name it and you can compare it to an industry benchmark—and then do something about it.

Show Me the Money

Now that we have discussed the two financial statements that can best be used to impact the management of your business, let's talk about that stuff that actually fuels your business. Let's talk about what it is that allows you to pay the rent, compensate your employees and turn on the lights in the morning.

Let's talk about cash.

Chapter 7
Understand—and Forecast—Cash Flow

"If you don't have the cash to pay yesterday's bills and to meet tomorrow's payroll, then your profitability really doesn't matter."

In business, cash is vital. To illustrate just how vital, I want to tell you a story. In February of this year, I ran into a friend at a Chamber of Commerce meeting. After exchanging pleasantries, I asked her the standard "how's business?" question.

"Oh, it's wonderful!" my friend replied and her body language told me she meant it. "I just received last year's financial statements this week."

"Tell me more," I replied.

"Well, my sales were up 25 percent," she said proudly. "And I know what you're thinking Jim, but my profits were up too. By 15 percent!"

"That's great," I congratulated her. She had had problems in the past, so I was happy to hear she had worked out the bugs, although a red flag went up with that last statement. While her profits had increased by 15 percent, they weren't keeping up with her 25 percent increase in sales. In other words, sales were growing faster than profits, meaning there was a leak somewhere.

"One problem however," she said, as if reading my mind. "I'm having more trouble paying my bills on time this year than last."

The Difference Between Profits and Cash

A few well-placed questions and her story came together. There is an old business adage that applies to this situation—maybe you've heard it:

"Profits are what you pay taxes on; cash is what you take home."

What this adage means is that *profit* is an accounting term while *cash* is that hard, green stuff that resides in your cash register and in your checking account. There is a big difference between the two, as my friend was learning the hard way. Which brings up another iconic adage:

"If you don't have enough cash to pay today's bills, then tomorrow doesn't matter."

Cash is the fuel that runs your business, while profitability is an accounting term used to settle your tax bill. Like your car, when your business' fuel runs out, it stops.

The words *cash flow* describe the flow of money (cash, checks, electronic debits and credits) in and out of your business. It is, in short, your checkbook, except that your checkbook only tells you how much cash you have today. It doesn't tell you why you have it, how much you'll have next month, or what you need to do to increase it.

The Three Giant Cash Suckers

My friend with the cash flow problem owns a light manufacturing company, replete with small business' three, sneaky giant suckers of cash: inventory, accounts receivable and equipment. Those three giant suckers of cash have two things in common:

1. When you fund them, they require cold-hard cash.

2. When you account for them, they don't immediately affect profitability, which is why they are sneaky. They're hiding from your P&L.

So, what happened to my friend's cash? It turned out that:

- She had increased her inventory significantly during the course of the year in order to satisfy her 25 percent increase in sales and the new customers that came with it. Funding inventory requires cash, but doesn't show up on the P&L.

- Her accounts receivable had also increased by 25 percent because it had no other choice, as it kept pace with the 25 percent increase in sales. Funding accounts receivable requires cash, but doesn't show up on the P&L.

- She had purchased a significant amount of computer equipment and software in order to keep her systems and controls on track with her increased sales. Funding capital expenditures requires cash, but it doesn't show up on the P&L.

This story paints a classic picture of how a profitable business can literally grow itself into trouble. If you're in a business where the three great suckers of cash are alive and well, and if your profitability increase doesn't keep up with your sales increase, this could happen to you.

Most successful businesses, the really, truly successful ones, learn to project cash flow. They don't want to be caught like my friend with her checking account bare. Their owners have learned that cash and profitability don't necessarily run hand in hand. They've also learned that while they can manage the operations of their business using their P&L and balance sheet, they need a third tool to manage their cash. Enter the rarefied world of generating cash flow projections.

Projecting Cash Flow

Cash flow projections do exactly what they say, i.e., they project future cash needs, just as budget projections project future profitability. Cash flow projections provide a peek into the future, and if that peek shows that you're going to be short of cash by July, then you've got to start doing something about it in June. Or, more likely, long before.

In essence, cash flow projections are designed to predict what will happen to your checkbook within a given period of time. What will your bank balance be two months from now? What position will you be in to pay your bills on time? Will you have more cash than you need? Will you have less?

Could my friend have done something about her cash flow problem if she had been projecting her cash flow and known a cash crunch was coming? The answer is an unqualified yes. She could have, for instance, postponed her capital expenditures. Or she could have leased the equipment instead of purchasing it. Alternatively, she could also have made the decision to maintain her inventory at a lower level; she could have promoted low-priced sales on her slow-moving inventory in order to trade it for cash, thus decreasing her need for cash; she could have offered cash discounts to her customers to speed up their payment; or she could even have worked her slow-paying accounts receivable harder in order to free up the cash required to fund those receivables. There are a myriad of things a business owner can do to generate cash if she knows in advance that a shortage is on the horizon.

Ask your accountant to help you generate a cash flow projection system for your business. If your accountant is a small business veteran, this will not be the first time he's been asked about cash flow. If he's incapable of setting one up, go back and review Chapter 1— you have the wrong accountant. In the process of developing your own cash flow projections, not only will you generate numbers that will aid you in running your business, you'll also learn everything you need to know about the ebb and flow of that hard, green stuff that's the lifeblood of your business.

In the process of teeing you up to generate your own cash flow projections, your accountant should also give you the option of preparing your projections for one day out, one week out, one month out or any combination thereof. Be aware that predictions for longer time periods than six months are likely to be fuzzier and less accurate than predictions for shorter time periods since cash needs can change so fast. Make your cash flow projections for six months out, and update them every month, always remaining six months out.

In summation, it's life-or-death important that every small business owner understand the concept behind measuring cash flow. No matter how small or uncomplicated your business happens to be, cash will always be king.

More Numbers

We've now discussed the three key financial statements required to run a successful, sophisticated business. A plethora of numbers is embodied in those statements, the combined meaning of which is not always understood. Welcome to the world of creating—and understanding—your business' key performance indicators.

Chapter 8
Create Your Key Indicators

"Besides using the key indicator report to manage decisions, its biggest advantage is keeping your key employees involved in the direction of the business."

Would you like to have a tool that helps keep your employees engaged and your business decisions on target? Of course you would.

Meet the key indicator report.

A key indicator report is, well, a report that details your business' key financial indicators. Also known as a key performance indicator report (or KPI report), key indicators are those numbers, ratios or percentages that you deem to be the most important measurements of your business. You'll select those key indicators yourself, usually six to 10 key numbers, percentages or ratios that are of particular interest to you as a business owner, and then have your bookkeeper or controller include the resultant report with your monthly financial statement package.

Certainly, these key indicators can change from year to year, as your focus changes and as your problem areas ebb and flow. You'll need to review the list annually and add or cull the individual indicators as your issues change. Nothing is sacred with the key indicators you select, although there are a number of them that are obviously more important than others. Gross sales, gross margin, inventory turn, accounts receivable DSO (days sales outstanding), current ratio and debt-to-equity are probably the most important to most businesses.

Besides using the key indicator report to manage decisions, its biggest advantage is keeping key employees involved in the direction of the business. After all, employees don't have to know how to read financial statements to understand key indicators. All they have to do is understand the individual key indicators themselves. Thus, the report is really one giant scorecard similar to, say, baseball. But instead of showing earned runs, home runs and strikeouts, this scorecard shows return on sales, gross margin and inventory turn, or whatever the business owner wants it to show.

The best way to describe a key indicator report is to show you one. Here's a sample key indicator report for Rubber Ducky Inc., followed by what might be your commentary to your employees if you owned this Ducky little company:

RUBBER DUCKY INC.
KEY INDICATOR REPORT FOR
THE MONTH OF APRIL, 2002

	Current Year	Prior Year
Profit for April	$14,000	$9,000
ROS – Year to Date	8.5%	6.3%
Sales for the Month	$155,000	$132,000
Website Sales	24,000	5,000
Current Ratio	1.8 to 1	1.6 to 1
Debt-to-Equity	.8 to 1	1 to 1
Inventory Dollars	$198,000	$190,000
Accounts Receivable	$185,000	$130,000
% Receivables over 60 days	12%	3%
Salaries & Wages as a % of Sales	22%	23%
Freight In	$3,500	$5,400

Deciphering the Key Indicator Report

After handing out this report to your employees, your comments might go something like this:

- **Profit for April:** "Good job, folks. Our ROS (return on sales) for April was 9 percent ($14,000 divided by $155,000) compared to last year's 6.8 percent ($9,000 divided by $132,000). Thus, as we grow, we continue our trend of becoming more efficient at turning a sales dollar into a profit dollar."

- **Sales for the Month:** "Nice job, sales department. Our sales in April were up 17 percent over the same month last year!"

- **Internet Sales:** "It's easy to see where most of our sales increase came from: the Internet. Is this a blip or will it be a continuing trend? Should we throw more marketing dollars at our website? How can we continue to leverage this new direction?"

- **Current Ratio:** "And the beat goes on. Chalk up another month of continuing improvement for our current ratio. Our banker is going to love us even more. How cool is this, watching our financial liquidity continue to improve."

- **Debt-to-Equity:** "Our creditors can now claim ownership of a slightly smaller portion of our company than they could a year ago."

- **Inventory Dollars:** "Nice job, Linda [who handles purchasing]. We sold more dollars this year than last on less inventory. That's a great trend, and our cash flow will be the biggest benefactor, along with the folks in the shipping and receiving department who have to handle any slow-moving inventory we don't sell."

- **Accounts Receivable:** "Oops, what's happening here? We have significantly more dollars in receivables than we do in April's sales. Meanwhile, if you look at last year's numbers, you can see we had approximately one month's sales in our receivables. That's what it should be if we were collecting our receivables in 30 days. Helen [the bookkeeper], can you explain what's going on here?"

- **Percentage of Receivables over 60 Days:** "Aha, we've just identified the AR (accounts receivable) culprit. We've got two large customers that are stringing us along. What's being done to get them back within terms? Helen, do I need to get involved in the collection process?"

- **Salaries & Wages as a Percentage of Sales:** "Good trend here folks. The improvement in this key indicator has been going on for six months now. Our decision at the beginning of the year to become more aware of this expense category is paying off. We've cut down on our overtime and yet, judging by our continuing ROS improvement, are not losing any efficiency as a result."

So you now have a general idea as to how to use a key indicator report as a management tool. In addition to providing you with the ultimate scorecard, the KPI report provides feedback to your employees who impact the numbers on your financial statements while providing tangible feedback to those who are responsible for making the numbers.

But to be helpful, that kind of information must be current. The same goes for the balance sheet, P&L, cash flow and KPI reports. What happens if the numbers on all those cool reports aren't immediately available to those who can learn from them? What happens if the numbers are stale? That's next.

Chapter 9
Get Your Financial Statements
Out on Time

"Approximately right now is better than exactly right later on."

As you might expect, the wise old sage of small business also has an adage to share on the topic of financial statement timing. It's no coincidence, by the way, that the wise old sage seems to have an adage for just about everything that small business folks do. That's because wise old sages have long since learned that small business problems are generic. It makes little difference what business or industry you're in; every problem you have is one that someone else has also had or is having.

The wise old sage's adage on the subject of the timing of month-end financial statements goes something like this:

"Approximately right now is better than exactly right later on."

What the wise old sage is saying here is that the quicker you can generate your month-ending, quarter-ending and year-ending financial statements, the better off your business will be. Quickness pays off because numbers, ratios and percentages, like cookies and bread, get stale with age. It's easier to do something about numbers that are one week old than it is to do something about those that are three weeks old.

Every Day Matters

Let's suppose, for instance, that your P&L regurgitates the fact that your gross margin came in at 25 percent last month, when it typically comes in at 35 percent. This 10 percent discrepancy is known as *margin shrink*, and it means that somewhere in your business you've sprung a leak. The leak could be due to such factors as employee theft, outsider theft, billing problems, shipping and receiving problems, or pricing problems. You need to find out why you're experiencing margin shrink from among this variety-pack of possible reasons and you need to find out now.

So what's the big rush? The big rush is that every day that goes by the trail gets colder. Plus, every day that goes by without the problem being corrected, the losses mount. Assuming you find that the numbers are accurate, i.e., that this isn't an accounting problem and you really are suffering from a case of acute margin shrink, then the heat from the problem intensifies. Now you're not only looking at *margin shrink*, you're looking at *profit shrink*. And *cash shrink*.

Most successful small businesses generate their monthly financial statements somewhere between the 15th and 20th working day of the following month. Unfortunately, this is too late. You should be generating them no later than the 10th working day of the month and, if you are willing to make one slight adjustment to the process, you could have the results even sooner. That adjustment is not to wait for your bank statement, never mind reconciling that bank statement to your checkbook. Assume the checkbook is correct, make whatever assumptions are necessary and then crank out your financials. When the bank statement does arrive, if there are small corrections to be made, you can make the necessary adjustments.

A word of warning here: Your bookkeeper, controller or chief financial officer (CFO) will likely squawk about this *approximately right* philosophy. And well they should. After all, most folks who make their living juggling numbers are fans of *exactly right*. Those people don't like adjusting numbers and they don't like explaining adjustments and justifying mistakes. But your job, in this case anyway, is to overcome their objections. You need numbers to manage your business and you need them as soon as you can get them. Tomorrow is too late. By comparison, a couple of minor bookkeeping or accounting adjustments pale in importance.

Most Fortune 500 companies with billions of dollars in annual sales can generate *approximately right* financial statements within four or five working days following the end of the month. If the big guys can do it, so can you.

There's another financial-related task that plays an integral role in any successful business without getting the credit it deserves. That task is receivable collection, or, stated another way, turning the money your customers owe you into the fuel that drives your business.

Chapter 10
Stay on Top of Your Receivables

"A customer is someone who buys your products and pays his bills within an agreed-upon time."

Are you aware that you and your banker have something in common? You are both in the money-lending business. The difference, of course, is that your banker lends money professionally and usually makes a profit on each transaction. Meanwhile, too many small business owners unwittingly lend money and none of them ever makes a profit on those transactions.

"That's not true," I hear you say.

I beg to differ. The term *net 30 days* really means *30 days of interest-free loans.*

When a customer buys your product and says "charge it", you are suddenly in the interest-free, money-lending business. After all, the customer has your widget and you don't have his money. Which means your customer is using something he hasn't paid for.

Okay, so the transaction can be good for you too, if 1) you've made a large enough profit on the sale and 2) your customer pays your invoice on time. All of which means that collecting the monies due is an integral part of the business cycle and just as important as everything else you do.

Oh, the irony of it all. We make heroes out of our sales people when they make the big sale. But the big sale doesn't do our company one iota of good unless the big collection is not far behind. In fact, big sales can lead to big failures when the big cash doesn't follow within a reasonable amount of time.

Someone Must Be Accountable

Every successful business needs someone dedicated to, and accountable for, the collection of receivables. In the early stages of the business that someone is usually you, the owner. In the later stages, that responsibility may be delegated to a bookkeeper, controller or chief financial officer. Whoever that person happens to be, he/she must be passionate about collecting monies due; first politely following up, then relentlessly hounding, and finally hauling the deadbeats to court.

Many of us love to recite the old *the customer is always right* mantra. Sure, that mantra makes sense, but before we give the customer what amounts to an interest-free loan, we must first define the word *customer*. A customer is someone who buys your products or services *and* pays his bills within an agreed-upon time.

After all, *accounts receivable* really represents our cash resting in someone else's hands. And since cash is what keeps our doors open, we need it in our bank account and not in our customers'.

Tips on Managing Your Receivables

Now that you understand the importance of converting receivables into cash, here is a collection of tips designed to help you improve the process:

- **What Gets Measured Gets Attention:** Outstanding receivables should be aged (a listing itemizing the status, i.e., age, of every outstanding receivable) at least once a month. This aging list should sit on either the boss' or the financial person's desk, a constant reminder of who is in possession of the business' cash. Procedures should be in place for every level of outstanding receivable over 30 days—say a polite phone reminder at 40 days, a second reminder at 50 days, a formal letter at 60 days, a call from the boss at 90 days, and then a collection service letter at 120 days, followed up by the collection agency itself at 150 days. Whatever timeframes you determine, make sure the procedure you establish is cast in stone.

- **Check Credit:** You can bet that your banker checked your credit before he lent you the bank's cash and, I suspect, the same was also true with your key vendors, especially the more professional ones. Remember, the granting of credit is a privilege to those on the receiving end. Grant your credit with care.

- **Establish Terms:** No sale should be made without first agreeing on credit terms. Terms must work for both parties. But remember, when a customer wants you to carry his receivables for long periods of time, that's your signature on the bank's guarantee. The structure of terms must, first and foremost, work for you.

- **Use a Standard Credit Application:** Design and use a standard credit application form. Look at some of those you've filled out for your vendors and select the format and content you like best. Every customer should have a credit application on file.

- **Evaluate All Credit Applicants:** Ask yourself these three questions before approving a credit application.

  1. Does this applicant have the ability to pay?
  2. Has he indicated by his past actions a willingness to pay on time?
  3. Can you make a reasonable profit on the account? If the answer to any of these three questions is no, cede the customer to your competition and move on.

- **Sales Contract:** Design a boilerplate sales contract, one that provides the legalese you need to collect your monies in court. Outline everything from payment terms to late payment charges to collection procedures. Officially signed sales contracts denote professionalism, and potential deadbeats will usually pay the professional businesses first.

- **Ask for a Financial Statement:** Don't be afraid to ask for a financial statement before shipping to a first-time customer. After all, your bank asked for one from you. Assumedly, so did some of your largest vendors.

- **Up-Front Money:** When in doubt with a first-time customer, or when a customer needs your products or services before you're able to complete a credit check, ask for money up front. Failing that, COD works too.

- **The Older the Receivable, the Less Likely the Collection:** Don't wait until your receivables are over 90 days to kick in your collection procedures. The sooner you pick up the slow-pays, the better.

- **Today Doesn't Mean Forever:** A customer's ability to pay on time changes as the fortunes of his company change. Don't brand a slow-pay as a slow-pay-forever. Instead, track his year-to-year progress and make sure your credit decisions are based on his latest performance. The inverse of this is also true. Today's good customer can be tomorrow's deadbeat. Don't assume that customers will always pay their bills on time.

- **Use a Collection Agency Only as a Last Resort:** Collection agencies are expensive, oftentimes charging up to 50 percent to collect your receivable. Also, collection agencies are not known for their impeccable manners when dealing with deadbeats; when using one you can usually kiss that customer goodbye forever.

- **No Pay, No Ship:** Don't ship to ongoing customers who consistently don't pay on time. After all, your good vendors wouldn't ship to you if you were a career slow-pay. In those cases where you determine that you absolutely, positively, must have the slow-paying customer's business, be sure to build the cost of carrying his receivables into the price of your service or product.

Finally, most small business grizzled veterans can walk into a business and, in short order, determine how professionally it's being managed by looking at its accounts receivable aging. If the aging is quickly produced and is kept in a conspicuous location, if it's neat and orderly and shows signs that someone is actively working it, and if whoever it is that's responsible for keeping it up-to-date is hovering nearby, anxious to explain why Acme Wood Supply has $1,000 in the over 60-day column, then that veteran will know that the business' receivables are in good hands.

The proof, as the old sage might say, is in the aging.

Untouchable Assets

Similar to accounts receivable, inventory is yet another asset that represents cash that you can't use. Until inventory is sold, billed and collected, it represents piles upon piles of your hard-earned cash sitting upon a shelf in the back of the warehouse. Until inventory is turned into cash it's no good to anyone, including your customers and, most of all, you.

Chapter 11
Manage Your Inventory or It Will Manage You

"Inventory is the most dangerous asset of them all!"

Are you familiar with the term *asset lending?* Or how about *asset-based lending?* For those of you who aren't, these two synonymous terms describe a lending technique that bankers use. The terms describe a financial transaction whereby the bank takes a lien on your business' assets as collateral for a loan. The two categories of a small business' assets most often employed in an asset-based lending transaction are accounts receivable and inventory.

There's an interesting difference between those two assets in the eyes of a banker. Typically, the bank will lend you an amount equal to 80 percent to 85 percent of your accounts receivable dollars, but only 40 percent to 50 percent of your inventory dollars. Why the difference? The bankers are aware that should your business encounter tough times, they would end up owning your assets. They could probably convert 80 percent to 85 percent of your receivables into cash but only 40 percent to 50 percent of your inventory.

Yep, those bankers have learned the lesson that their small business customers have taught them over the past century or so: Inventory is the most dangerous asset of them all. This lesson explains why inventory has a much lower collateral value than accounts receivable.

Inventory: The Biggest Killer Asset of Them All

Diamondback rattlesnakes are less dangerous than inventory. At least you can hear a rattlesnake, you can see it as it prepares to strike, and, if you're lucky, you can beat it to death with a stick.

Not so with inventory. Slow-moving inventory is the greatest cash-sucking, profit-draining, killer asset of them all. Unsold inventory sits on your shelves and collects dust. And interest. And as it sits, it gets older, and yellower and deadlier, until its owner discovers that too much of his cash is tied up in shelf after shelf of dust-ridden, obsolete inventory. That's cash that could be used to pay his bills, or meet payroll, or that he could take home at the end of the year. His motley collection of obsolete widgets certainly won't pay those bills or help him meet payroll. Whereupon the creditors move in and the employees move out, and all those dusty, obsolete widgets bring the house down.

The good news about inventory is that there is money to be made in the handling of it, for those detail-oriented folks who are comfortable taking risks. For the rest of the world, Russian roulette offers better odds.

The late Sam Walton had to be the greatest attention-to-detail business owner of them all. Walmart, Sam's company, learned how to manage its inventory better than any other business in the world.

(Okay, so Amazon may have caught up.) Look where it got them. Walmart ships, receives, stores and distributes its inventory like it's made of gold, which, in effect, it is.

Tips on Handling Inventory

You say that despite this not-so-subtle warning, you are either going to start an inventory-related business or already have? Here is a collection of tips to help you manage your inventory properly:

- **Take Frequent Physical Inventories:** Are you aware that the accuracy of your gross margin number on your P&L cannot be validated until you've taken a physical inventory? That's right. In those months, or quarters, when you don't take a physical inventory, your gross margin, and thus your business' bottom line, is only a guesstimate. This means that you're taking a chance trusting your numbers in those months, which further means your net profit just might be a net loss.

  If, for instance, an employee starts walking off with your most expensive widgets in June and continues to do so throughout the summer and fall, and if you don't take a physical inventory until December 31, then you won't have any idea that your inventory has been shrinking until the middle of January when your financial statements are completed. Or at least the shrinkage won't show up in your numbers, unless your thief is considerate enough to leave an accounting entry behind, which would be a debit to *expense theft account* and a credit to *inventory*. (This is supposed to be a joke; hopefully you don't have an expense theft account.)

The best inventory-managing small businesses take monthly physical inventories. As a result, when the P&Ls come out, those businesses know that their gross margin numbers are absolutely, positively correct. If monthly inventories are impractical, then quarterly inventories will do. But that's the outside limit. Six months is too long.

In addition to keeping tabs on your inventory, you want to make sure that it's treated as an asset and doesn't become a liability. A few tips:

- **Track the Turn:** *Inventory turn* is a number that represents the frequency with which inventory turns over. It's arrived at by dividing the cost of goods sold (from the P&L) by the year's average inventory—the year's beginning inventory plus the current inventory divided by 2. The higher the inventory turn, the more sales dollars the business has in relation to the size of its inventory. The result of a high inventory turn is a more positive cash flow.

- **Utilize the Necessary Software:** An accurate financial accounting system and paperwork flow is the #1 key to handling inventory successfully. Most entry-level accounting systems aren't capable of delivering a professional inventory tracking system. If an inventory-friendly software upgrade is on your mind, remember that it takes six months or so from the time you begin investigating a new system until it's up and running smoothly. Don't wait until your current system is gasping its last breath before you begin planning the upgrade.

- **Make Inventory a Priority:** If you, the owner, don't assume direct accountability for inventory yourself, at least make it your personal priority to oversee the progress in the systems and controls that your business needs. Also, be sure and set goals for inventory levels. If your employees know that your eyes are glued to the dollars tied up in your inventory, then fiscal awareness will become a part of your culture.

- **Divided It Falls:** Divide your inventory into small, manageable pieces, allowing for easier tracking and quicker reference. This will also make your inventory lists more user-friendly, especially for the folks whose job it is to sell it. Then get involved in setting mini-goals for those manageable pieces. Identify your most-wanted-to-dump inventory and make heroes out of the people who sell it.

- **Man the Battle Stations:** Make sure there are good employees at the inventory-handling corners—receiving and shipping. Train those employees thoroughly, not only on their own duties, but on related bookkeeping functions as well. Most inventory shrinkage problems can be identified, traced and resolved at the bookkeeping level.

- **Take the Hit When It Occurs:** Most bankers I know don't like inventory hits (write-downs) that accumulate but aren't taken, especially when inventory is serving as the bank's collateral. Sure, substantial inventory write-downs can make the current financials look ugly, but don't postpone taking the painful ones. Postponing them may rescue the current year's P&L, but the pain will compound when the truth finally comes out.

- **Hit the Delete Key:** Finally, when in doubt, cancel the order. Your vendors might scream today, but that's a better option than having to eat the inventory tomorrow.

There *is* good news on the subject of inventory. The opportunities to improve profitability by the efficient handling of it are boundless. Inventory isn't gray, like marketing, or steeped in hypothesis, like sales. It's there to touch, and feel, and count, and the impact of inventory when it's exchanged for cash is instantaneous, and, oh so pleasurable.

Where Do You Go from Here?

I've now shared 50 years of hard-earned lessons about the value of financial statements. Hopefully, you've gotten the point that understanding your financial statements is an integral part of building a successful company.

Assuming you've assimilated the lessons herein, what comes next? Will it be business as usual or is something new in the cards?

Chapter 12
One More Thing Before
We Part Company

"When things aren't going the way you would like them to go, trying harder doesn't always work. The only thing that does always work is to try differently, i.e., to make a fundamental change in the way you conduct your business."

Let's suppose, just for a moment, that you've encountered a lesson or two in this book that struck a resounding chord. "Aha," you chortled, smashing the table with your fist. "This makes sense. I think I'll do something about it."

Hopefully you've learned by now that you wouldn't be successful in this vocation if you weren't disposed to doing something about whatever needs to get done. After all, getting things done is what small business people are famous for. But what exactly will you do? Will you commit to simply trying harder, or will you make a commitment to institute a fundamental change in the way you do business?

Well, the wise old sage has an adage for this situation too:

"When things aren't going the way you would like them to go, trying harder doesn't always work. The only thing that does always work is to try differently, i.e., to make a fundamental change in the way you conduct your business."

We're Muckers, Diggers and Bulldogs

Sadly, when most small business owners have problems, they grit their teeth, hitch up their pants and, by God, they work harder. And then harder. After all, that's what got them where they are. If they have to scrounge another ten hours out of a week, then so be it; their home life and hobbies will have to suffer. If you're like most small business owners, you've done it before.

But there comes a time in the life of most businesses when trying harder simply doesn't work anymore. When that's no longer enough, we need to try something new, something different. We need to work smarter, not harder.

Changing Your Financial Ways

Here are a select few of the many options to consider in order to make the above-described fundamental change in the way you manage the financial aspects of your business:

- **Upgrade Your Bookkeeper:** The bookkeeper you have now may not be capable of projecting cash flow, deciphering your balance sheet or giving you advice on collecting your receivables. You have two choices: 1) train her or 2) replace her. To replace her will probably cost another $7,000 per year in salary to upgrade the position, not to mention the cost of training her replacement. Training your existing bookkeeper will cost appreciably less, but you need to be sure that the training will take root.

- **Hire a Controller:** Sooner or later, a growing business will reach the point where it needs a controller, the next step up from bookkeeper. Tack on at least another $10,000 or so a year in annual salary over the price of a good bookkeeper.

- **Hire a CFO:** You say you already have a controller? Then your next step is to hire a CFO with a CPA or similar designation. A capable CFO should be able to do it all, including working with the bank and even overseeing most of those mind-numbing human resource issues that give small business owners indigestion. Tack on another $25,000 a year over the cost of a controller.

- **Find a Financial Mentor:** This person could be your tax advisor, but there may be others out there who qualify. Budget $2,500 or so a year and then schedule your financial consultant/advisor/mentor at the end of every month or quarter to review your financials and make his recommendations. Forcing yourself to follow his advice will also provide you with a taste of accountability.

- **Upgrade Yourself:** There is plenty of training available for delving more in depth into the lessons we've talked about in this book. You'll find that training on the web, at your local SBDC or at your local community college or university. Certainly, it will take time and yes, time is money, but misdirection will cost even more money. If you're going to get serious about taking your business to the next level, upgrading yourself is the most obvious place to start. Besides, if you eventually want to take your business to the next level, you're going to have to do this upgrading sometime. Sooner is better than later.

Conclusion

If you've learned one thing from this book, I hope that it's that numbers, as cold and impersonal as they may be, drive the direction of your business. Don't get me wrong. Numbers don't actually drive your business—that's what you do. But they do drive the decisions you make, which, in turn, drive the direction your business takes. In short, without numbers, you and your business are rudderless.

It makes no sense, none at all, that small business owners should endure the time and expense of generating numbers and then not use them. Let's face it, everyone else uses numbers to steer their organizations. Professional football teams use numbers to determine which players are going to play on Sunday and how much they're going to pay them. Financial advisors use numbers to decide which stocks to buy and how much they're going to pay for them. Even writers, words-driven people like me, use numbers to determine how many words we're going to write, how long it will take to write them and the odds of getting paid for them.

If so many other types of businesses put numbers to work for them, why wouldn't we?

Most small business owners are quick to tell us that it's their customers who pay the bills, and it's their employees who find those customers and keep them coming back. But it's numbers that identify who your good customers are, and it's numbers that tell you whether or not your customers allow you to make a profit. Numbers will also identify how many employees you need in the first place, how much you can pay them and what you can afford to have them do.

Yes, small business is all about numbers. Here's hoping that yours are correct, timely, and of course, black.

Note to the Reader

There's just no way to build and maintain a successful business without knowing how to interpret and use the critical information contained in your financial statements. I hope the information I've presented helps you right your financial ship if you're in trouble or makes sure you never drift off course if things are going well.

This book, originally published under another title in 2002, has been my personal favorite of the six books I've authored. I say favorite because I've received more positive feedback from the 10,000 or so copies that have been distributed than I have from the other five books combined. I include in this appraisal the *Small Business for Dummies* book I co-wrote, which has sold hundreds of thousands of copies in a dozen different languages.

It seems that today's small business owners and entrepreneurs prefer their lessons in short bursts, similar to the way they like their news and their coffee. To see what I mean, compare this small book, which is a one-hour read, to the typical 200-page nonfiction business book requiring four to five hours to read. If you could learn the same lessons and save three hours in doing so, which option would you take?

When I visit with small business owners and CPAs around my community, I often see the original book perched on their book shelf or somewhere close to their desk. That visual never ceases thrill me, as easy access and frequent referral is what I was hoping for when I wrote it.

This book is intended to improve your financial proficiency and, by extension, your business. If it has, or is, and you want to make my day, please email me at jim.schell5@gmail.com and give me your feedback. I'd love to hear from you.

Jim Schell

Hey there, and congratulations on reaching the end of this book—you are now prepared to better understand financial statements and make your mark on the world. But before then, I would like to give you a chance to help me, and to help yourself in the process as well.

Reviews are the backbone of many successful books and, more importantly, a chance for you to have a direct impact on the content that I create in the future. I highly recommend that you take several moments to leave a review. I will personally read all of them and take them into careful consideration for future releases. You are helping to ensure that I create amazing content in the future that you will love.

Go to lightsonpublishing.com/feedback to leave a review—don't worry about length, spelling, grammar, or anything else for that matter, as the simple effort of leaving a review is what will allow me to continue to help you in the future.

52749775R00053

Made in the USA
San Bernardino, CA
09 September 2019